Inspiring Ancient Yoga Teaching

Happy is the man who knows his mind
Happier is the man who opens his mind
Knowing his destiny, there are but a few of his kind.

Inspiring Ancient Yoga Teaching

INSPIRATIONAL AND MOTIVATIONAL WORDS OF WISDOM

Vincent G. Harford

First published 2010 by
LINDEN PUBLISHING SERVICES
Dublin • Ireland

Copyright © Vincent G. Harford 2010

ancientyogateachings@hotmail.com

A catalogue record for this book is available from the British Library. All rights reserved. No part of this publication may be reproduced, stored in a retrieval system or transmitted in any form or by any means, electronic, mechanical, photocopying, recording or otherwise, without the prior, written permission of the publisher.

This book is sold subject to the condition that it shall not, by way of trade or otherwise, be lent, resold, hired out, or otherwise circulated without the publisher's prior consent in any form of binding or cover other than that in which it is published and without a similar condition, including this condition, being imposed on the subsequent purchaser.

The author has received only positive feedback for the pieces in this book, it is the intension of the author to offer information of a general nature and in the event you use any of the information in this book, which is your constitutional right, the author and the publisher assume no responsibility for your actions.

1 3 5 7 9 10 8 6 4 2

ISBN 978 1453870365

Set in 11 on 14.5 Diotima by Susan Waine
Printed in USA

Contents

A word from the author	7
About the author	9
Acknowledgements	12
Introduction	13
Rekindle This Old Art	15
Intuition	18
Meditation Definition	20
The Illusion Of Wealth	21
Are You Being Tricked?	22
Magic Wishes	25
What Direction Are You Going?	28
Bring Only Good News	30
As The Mist Clears	33
The Forgotten Knight	35
Adjust Your Thinking Ways	37
The Imposters	38
What Map Are You Reading?	41
Money – The Wise Man's View	43
The Solution Is Obvious	44
Use Your Instructional Manual	45
Where Is Norman?	47
Goodness	51
What If...?	53
Make A Real Change	55
The Keys To Freedom	56
Zen Riddle	58
Set Yourself Free	59
News, News, News	61
Fickle	62
Money	63
Are You Trying Too Hard to Succeed?	65

The Destiny of Man?	67
True Grit	68
The Housewife	71
Your Wish	73
It's Never My Fault	75
Wisdom From Within	78
There Are Some	80
The Wisdom In Words	82
Heaven's Game	85
The Magic of Ireland	87
Get Out Of Your Prison	89
Hope	91
Who Tells Them They Have Flaws?	92
It's Not All About Me	95
Never Ever	97
Discover Your Youth	98
Don't let Your Thought Restrict You	101
The Makings Of A Man	103
Meditation Speaks on our Culture	104
Make The Change	106
The Cause Of Confusion	109
If You Were A Child	111
Seek Fulfilment	113
Where is the Real You?	115
Billy	116
Make The Right Connection	120
The Rat Race	121
There Is	123
The Wizard	124
Words To Enlighten	126
Defintions Of Words Used In This Book	127

A word from the Author

I DIDN'T WRITE this book. At least, I didn't write it in the conventional sense. To me it was almost as if it were dictated by a tiny voice from within. Many people ask me about the source of the material but that would be a story in itself and a very interesting one, too. I could probably write another book on that subject alone. This book contains only a sample of the transcribing and I have many more pieces on an array of topics and in various styles such as riddles, Zen, tongue twisters, proverbs, sayings, anti-war, rap, education and prayer, all of which are very informative and inspirational.

When you are reading or studying the various pieces featured in this book it is highly recommended that at some point you read them aloud and have others read them aloud to you. Many people have remarked that by doing this during readings at different healing and prayer meetings it seems to help the listener hear the words and also feel the strong emotional content imbedded in the piece. Some have described this feeling as the very essence of the piece resonating and touching them inside. It is often quite amazing to witness adults shed a tear as they listen, almost transfixed, to the core meaning of what is being read. People often describe the writings as a treasure trove of wisdom.

Each piece was transcribed by the author from a state of meditation. The majority of them are in verse and each one is a complete lesson in itself. If you in your heart seek a deeper meaning or purpose to life or if you want to explore what could be your destiny then this information may provide many of the answers. The author has been studying yoga philosophy for almost 40 years.

I do hope that you enjoy this book, and that you will find inspiration and guidance which may be appropriate to your personal situation. Although I have a lifelong interest in this field I would not consider myself a world authority on the subject and I welcome any feedback that you may have. Please e-mail me at ancientyogateachings@hotmail.com .

About the Author

MY INTEREST in yoga and yoga philosophy began when I was nineteen with a book on ESP (extra sensory perception). Part of the book mentioned so-called yoga masters who, it was said, could perform extraordinary feats far beyond the limitations of a normal man. For example, some were able to be immersed in water for up to two hours without breathing. Then there were those who, similar to the wizards of old, could see into the future and had great understanding and a huge appreciation of life, the real destiny and purpose of mankind. This fascination started me on a path that today, 40 years later, is even stronger and has resulted in the publication of this book.

As I near sixty, I can reflect on the many great lessons and experiences that I have had and just like many others, some I have learned the hard way. I always had a burning desire to follow this path, which at times has caused some conflict and turmoil with those closest to me. I can now look back and realize the errors that I have made and wonder if we are sometimes put through experiences such as sorrow, turmoil, stress, depression, anxiety, frustration, loneliness, happiness, joy, love, fulfillment and respect in order to help us understand and appreciate life?

In 1998, aged 48, I started to develop a health issue. It continued to get worse for the next five or six years until it was finally diagnosed as Parkinson's disease. During the following two years my condition deteriorated to the extent that I finally could not cope at work and had to take early retirement. Primarily, this ailment slurred my speech, making it very difficult to communicate and my physical movements slowed down considerably.

On my retirement I had time to research this disease and received a lot of help from friends. I also attended medical experts, healers and nutritionists, and continue to do so to this day. Through major adjustments in my diet, medication, and healing therapies I have experienced a lot of improvement. Perhaps with a little bit of luck I can continue to improve and one day I may make a full recovery.

As I was out of a job I began writing some days if I was well enough. This started with a small urge which grew in a matter of weeks, almost compelling me to write. On days when I felt unwell it would take the form of my barely audible whispering dictation to Lorraine who would sit and type with great patience, trying hard to interpret my garbled, muffled and barely audible voice. At the same time, my health issue was compounded and at times deteriorated as a result of other issues but through all of this, these words of inspiration gave me great hope and encouragement at times when it felt like I was being bombarded from all sides. It's a bit ironic but some of the most extraordinary pieces were produced at some of those times when I was under most pressure with financial, health and family issues.

I always commenced each session without any topic, just a blank sheet. The light would be turned down and usually once I had relaxed the words began appearing in my mind: often a short string of words appeared and with great effort I would try to dictate them to Lorraine. I was only aware of the few words I was dealing with at each moment. Then after the session Lorraine would read it back and I would be amazed that it was a complete story, usually in verse.

Acknowledgements

I would like to sincerely thank all those individuals who encouraged me so much to make these writings available to the public. There are far too many to mention by name but I would like to thank them for showing such appreciation for the insights that it kept me focused and helped me persist with the transcribing.

I would also like to give a very special thank you to Lorraine who assisted and helped me with day to day matters when my health was at its worst. She also gave me endless help with dictation and typing when I was severely incapacitated and voiceless as a result of Parkinson's disease, without which I could not have coped.

I want to give a special thank you to my mother Muriel and Lorraine who each week after the Sunday roast would review my latest pieces and consistently insisted that I should publish this book. They both had so much belief that their whole attitude gave me great strength to continue the transcribing particularly during times when my health was declining and I often found it hard to cope with simple everyday matters. I took great encouragement from both their attitude and the wisdom embedded within the writings.

Here too I want to thank Dr Tony Quinn and Martin Forde. Around 2004 my health began to seriously deteriorate and they both put in a huge amount of work researching my illness and guiding me through those dark and worrying times. Around 2008 Dr Quinn developed a health regime for me and now after two years on the program I have improved so that I am now beginning to enjoy a reasonable state of health and let us all hope it continues to improve. I very much appreciate the marvellous work you have done for me.

Introduction

THESE MYSTICAL WORDS are truly a form of inspiration and should be viewed with respect. You may find that some of them were written almost with you in mind and once the advice and guidance in these extraordinary works are understood it may help give you a whole new perspective and a new insight into yourself and the direction your life is going. It might also be useful to allow you to take control of the various aspects of your life.

Can you just imagine if you could begin to relate to your spirit? Consider the difference it could make in your life. It has often been said that sometimes we live our lives like headless chickens, filling our lives with the wrong tasks, the wrong job and the wrong relationships, etc. Far too often we spend our lives making choices and decisions that are more like guesswork, rather than having any real direction or guidance in them. So, if you were to start making decisions based on wisdom, would you then have an extraordinary life? Then issues such as fulfilment, joy, appreciation, health, happiness and a sense of achievement are likely to dominate and fill your life so there would be no space left for doubt, self-pity, feeling sorry for yourself or blaming others for your troubles.

Therefore, if you want to live a life that is truly blessed this may be the key; rather than being a victim of your circumstances you could find the path to your true destiny and live your life to its full potential and this could give you a whole new appreciation of Life, yourself, your spirit, and indeed, God.

Rekindle This Old Art

THE MODERN understanding of meditation can be misconstrued. To some, it can mean anything from staring at the flame of a candle for hours on end to sitting in a yoga posture, making your mind go blank, or being in some form of abstract trance. But in fact, you could say the essence of meditation is living according to the direction of your spirit.

Meditation may also be described as true knowledge, wisdom, or spiritual guidance. It is part of our true essence but in recent times it has fallen out of fashion. Man's ability to meditate, over time, has virtually been lost. It is similar to man choosing not to use one of his limbs: it would eventually be unable to function as intended and have to be retrained or reprogrammed. So, we all have the ability to meditate; all we need are the proper teachings to rekindle this remarkable talent. Perhaps it is now time to revive this old art and soon meditation will be back in fashion.

Todays 'in' things are clothes, cars, houses, money, etc. People today are too often judged by these accessories, but a real man operates from his source and is guided by the spirit and meditation. In other words, the spirit dictates and directs his destiny. This may not be apparent to the average man as these concepts may be just outside his understanding. The enlightened man may possess all the trimmings of his culture but his priority is to take guidance from his spirit. The meditation way of life is truly one to be cherished and nurtured. So you could view meditation as the intrinsic core of man.

To follow one's destiny is to take guidance from your very soul. What you feel in the deepest part of your heart can be one of the ways your spirit tries to connect with you. A hunch, premonition, feelings, intuition, these can be moments of enlightenment and, when nurtured properly, can all be forms of inspiration and should be treated with the respect they warrant.

The wise man realises the difference between wisdom and idle thought. He has taken the trouble to nurture the path to his destiny and is not tricked or persuaded to pursue goals which are not part of his destiny. Choosing to walk his golden path, he is not left wanting or lacking anything: he knows only emptiness is be found in pursuing falseness in the form of making lots and lots of effort but going nowhere, just like the hamster running and endlessly rotating on the wheel but not getting anywhere.

Typically we can have an apparently very busy life filled with endless activities, pursuing what we think is our destiny. Chasing schedules, plans and desires, just like the hamster on the wheel, we can often end up simply going around in circles, the result being that we can end up a square peg in a round hole.

To find our true purpose or our perfect role all we have to do is take guidance and direction from our true essence which can be found in the deepest part of our heart.

So rather than just listening to our thoughts we could consider going with our feelings and hunches – this may even lead us to the greatest quest of all, our true destiny.

INTUITION

*We have all heard the word hundreds of times; we all know what it means.
When you read this piece, you will probably find you will become more aware
of it and take note of its guidance.*

Use Intuition to Make Decisions

What is intuition? Could it show you your mission?
Could it be something divine?
For if you just pause, it would show you the cause
To get your life more in line

If you seek direction and a stronger connection
And are willing to take advice,
Then consider intuition, maybe as a premonition,
Which is really very nice?

We all know it, and we can all grow it
For it often comes in bunches.
We feel it in our heart, just like a little dart
That we recognize as hunches

Usually it can pulsate, at a very gentle rate,
Other times, it can come as a shock.
It may come with a feeling, often while you're dealing
And give you a little knock

It can give you news, when you have to choose
Or when there are decisions to make.
It will give you the edge, so that you won't hedge
The choices you're to take

It's not very strange, as it tries to arrange
Your life in perfect order.
It is there each day, trying to show you the way
And of dangers it will warn you

It is a plan we were given, before we left heaven
Setting out on our mission
When we were told, 'Just let it all unfold'
And all we have to do is listen.

It can be hard to use, if you're too confused,
It's important to respect it.
So when you're in a jam, just stay very calm
And it comes when you least expect it

So sometimes intuition may come in a vision
Or a tiny little voice.
It may come as a feeling when you are needing
To make the perfect choice

Meditation Definition

Meditation is information obtained from the spirit. It is often described as original, as it is not copied from a book, another person, society, or culture. It is original, because it is not conceived from memory, but from a source that could be considered a higher source or higher intelligence.

The information is usually advice, direction, or perhaps some very useful information on any given subject, such as health, work, and so on. It can offer very useful advice, recommending hobbies that have extra benefits, such as exercise, weight training, and nutrition, associating with the right people and doing the right job that's meant for you. So you are put in the right job and then in turn, you meet the perfect people and situations to educate you in the best way possible.

You could say meditation is a way of life or at least it gives the perfect advice and directions to you, which then enables you to have the perfect life. In fact, you could say 'The Perfect Life' is simply a result of going with the meditation directions and that is it, in a nutshell.

The Illusion of Wealth

What purpose has wealth? Does it fill your day?
Does it cloud your mind and lead you astray?

Does it fill your heart with love and compassion
Or does it tell you these feelings are not in fashion?

Do you seek riches and wealth without a cause?
Perhaps if you do, you might take a pause

If you seek riches before you have health
You must find your heart, for then you have wealth

Your health is the space between your mind and heart,
It's a place where inspiration will give you a start

Should you fill your life with ideas so strange?
It confuses your heart so you must rearrange

So clear all this baggage out of the way
Make space for the magic so it comes to stay

To take the wrong road just leads to confusion
So your heart gives directions for you to use them

If you are caught by cares and troubles
Make space for your heart, it will burst these bubbles

Travel your right path and your cares get lighter
And as you go further your future gets brighter

ARE YOU BEING TRICKED?

There are times when you may find that events are not going your way and you may feel somewhat caught in a rut. Rather than sitting at home feeling sorry for yourself and just hoping your life gets better, here is some excellent advice; all you need to do is take a little action. Pin this to your mirror and read it every morning when you get up.

Are You Being Tricked?

If you are troubled and restless
And you couldn't really care less,
You might want more pep in your step.
There is no need to be sad
Or feel really bad
There are facts that you should accept

For it's your thoughts that cover
And your life they smother,
Choking your very essence.
You may feel you want to escape
By taking a long break
Well, here are some important lessons

New hobbies invest in
Take on challenges you're best in
Put some new ideas into your life.
Develop lots of new pleasures
These can be treasures
For this will dissolve all the strife

Then your life is much fuller
Filled with variety and colour
So there is no time for 'poor me'.
As you grow in self-esteem
Your life will then seem
To be the way it ought to be

To dissolve all bad habits
It's like a magician with rabbits
There are endless tricks you can do.
For it is always the same
Bad habits are to blame
Maybe it's time you started anew

So now you can see
You can really be free
If you think you are caught in a rut.
Use some good lifelines
For isn't it about time
You just got yourself off your butt?

Don't let your thoughts mislead you,
For they will just deceive you,
Sending your life into hell.
So turn your life around
For you have just found,
The quickest way to make your life really swell

Don't ever accept defeat
Jump back on your feet
And get up early each morning.
Just do the right things,
For this always brings
Adventures and a whole new dawning

WISE SAYING
Maybe at the moment your spirit lies dormant
And craves for your attention
To bring you good advice and a life that is very nice
And take you out of detention?

MAGIC WISHES/PRAYER

The whole concept of prayer has different meanings for different people as indeed, so too, has the whole concept of how to pray. Different cultures have many versions and interpretations of what prayer is. This piece might help shed some light on this divine and powerful asset. Even if you don't pray you now, you may decide to take it up when you read this.

Magic Wishes / How to Pray

If you ever wished, you may be surprised to know
Did you wish in your heart, and where did your wish go?

How far can your mind reach?
Or are your wishes just empty speech?

So to learn the secret of this great art
All you need is to make a new start,

The key that will unlock this magician
Is first, cease all your crazy wishing!

The list of wishes that you have got
May not be what will improve your lot.

What you think you need so much
May not be right for you to touch

For all your wants may not be wholesome
And you might end up pretty lonesome. ☞

So if your wishes the magic has missed
Take much more care as you write your list

You may think money will improve your lot
And you omit the friends that you have got.

So is your life just chasing useless gold?
Take note of this secret that you have been told

Did you come to this Earth to collect pearls and diamonds?
When it's your spirit you should be mining?

Do you fill your life with foolish tasks?
Are these the duties that God asks?

Is it not time for you to see the joke
And finally take off this masquerading cloak?

So if you make wishes from this hazy state
To avoid further confusion it may be best to wait

To wish for guidance should be top of your list
So ask the magician to take you out of that mist

Then the path you should follow begins to arise
And when you travel it you start to get wise

To follow your destiny is your heart's desire
So cease all wishes that take you into the mire.

Seek out true guidance from your heart
Then you have made that brand new start

Now if you desire to be at your best
Begin by making the right request

WISE SAYING
The road you have travelled has its valleys and hills
And life gets tough when it's time to pay those bills.
What can you do when you think you're in a jam?
You make the one move and stick to the plan

What Direction is Your Life Going?

Like the donkey pursuing the carrot it can never reach,
Can you see the illusion or are you hard to teach?

You may chase rainbows, it can be your desire.
If you stay on this path, it takes you more into the mire

There is no path so sweet as the ones that's for you
And when you choose to travel it, your life will change too

The path to heaven is but one little step at a time
And don't expect these steps to be in a straight line

To find this mystical path, you must abandon thought
For then your true destiny, you have just sought

It's not the way you think or expect it to be
For divine inspiration does not come from the 'me'

So throw away your map and how you want life to unfold
And follow your spirit, now you have been told

Like crossing the river on steps not seen
Except for the next stone, as you cross the stream

As you live your life, do you, let your spirit guide you?
For this is the reason God put it inside you

What motivates you in the goals that you seek?
Are they divine and godly or are you too weak?

Are you wasting your life, are you going insane?
Do you forget the place from whence you came?

If you want to fill your life with all that is right
Step off that dark path and seek out the light

To give your life a purpose and a worthwhile meaning,
Just forget all your plans and stop all you're scheming

Is it not time you took stock of your life
Or are you more keen, to continue the strife?

BRING ONLY GOOD NEWS

I have a friend who has the rare ability to make you feel good every time you meet him. I don't think he realizes what he does or how he does it but I have figured him out. His secret is he never gossips or speaks ill of anyone. In fact, he sees only goodness in everyone and is forever talking about people and their great talents and achievements. He is the sort of fellow you could listen to for hours. The result of being in his company is you always feel great and maybe inspired. However, we all know people who do exactly the opposite – you know, when you see them coming your way, you might cross the street to avoid them because they constantly complain and whine about everything under the sun. Now, which camp do you belong to?

Bring Only Good News

To dwell on your thoughts can lead you into a rut
To dwell on your worries can give you a knot in your gut

To talk about gossip and to repeat bad news
Puts your mind in a spin and makes you confused

To speak ill of others is not recommended
It darkens your mind, for it's yourself you have offended

So if you are being foolish and you commit such a sin
It's time to cease these habits, because they can never win

As you meet and greet a friend or a foe
Here are some words of wisdom, which you ought to know

To bring good tidings and only good news
Is a guaranteed way to dissolve all the blues

And rather than clouding and causing a haze,
You then are creating much brighter days

So if you have been in the habit of giving folks an earful
Far better to bring news that makes them more cheerful

Should it be your intention to brighten others' lives,
Tell them only good stories, and then you have become very wise

Everybody likes to enjoy or have a special day
And wouldn't you be the lucky one, if you made it better in some way

Don't spread rumours, which tarnish a poor soul
Far better to stop the slander, take on a real manly role

So if you have a habit of gossiping and you really want a cure
Just live on the bright side and take your head out of that sewer

Are you motivated by jealousy? Is your attitude a bit sour?
Are you part of that mob and do you run with that shower?

So clean up your vocals, use only words that are sweet
Then when you meet friends, give them a big hearty greet

Let the one who is without sin, cast the first stone
Rather than stirring up trouble, it's far better left alone

If you want to be known for being honest and gallant,
Use only the right words and show them that you have talent

Can you stand forth and honestly look others in the eye?
And if you can't see any goodness, you better ask yourself why

What we tend to see in others is only ourselves reflected
If you are constantly complaining, you will know your thinking is defective

So do the words you speak, make the right impression
Or do they cause and create a state of depression?

Do you consistently blame others, for all your mistakes?
Is it never your fault? Is it not just honesty that it takes?

Do you tend to see yourself as the unfortunate victim?
When you were given opportunities, was it you who did restrict them?

Are you always thinking about how much you can gain?
Maybe you should really think about others and stop being a pain

Do you go to church on Sunday, do you ask for forgiveness
Then continue to put your nose in other people's business?

So if you want to be the one that wants to do what is right,
Be fair and compassionate it is then you become that shining knight

CULTURE PIECES

These kinds of writings I call 'culture' pieces. They are observations or almost predictive pieces of information and point out those blatant flaws in our society that we may be overlooking. Please note that where the words 'man' and 'mankind' are used they refer to all of humankind that is, both man and women.

As The Mist Clears

As the mist clears, there is a sight to behold
As man will realize, the falsehoods he has been sold

The leaders who have taught you and led you astray
Are now getting close to the end of their day

As man realizes the gifts that he has within
A whole new life will start to begin

The expression of freedom has been subdued for too long
And the wise man realizes that this is so wrong

Now it is time for this information to unfold
And every soul on earth will be told

Sailing out of the fog and into a clearing
You will learn the news that you find endearing

☞

Just like the dawning of creation, when man was anew
God entered into the world, for he knew what to do

So speak with strength and speak with power
And to hide these secrets, you will no more

Leap forward with courage and take up this mission
For this is the world that you have been wishing

―⁂―

WISE SAYING
You hear the advice, are you near the advice,
Could you hold it dear, the advice?
You seek the advice, you read the advice
But it's really nice to take the advice

The Forgotten Knight

Old English was a man full of character and wit
At the gates of the castle he often chose to sit

To tell of his past and who he had met
The tale he told, you would never forget

Here was a man who had class and indeed
He could read you like a book, it was him you should heed

Never to be forgotten, for when he spoke
The room fell silent; this was no joke

He would speak of diamonds, rubies and pearls
Reminding us of his family who all seemed to be earls.

A hearty welcome, gesturing to all who came his way
Telling the people to slow down and enjoy their stay

Old Jake was his horse, his pal and his steed
Many taverns they visited but Jake had no need

Waiting in the yard for his master to return
To tread those green pastures he longed for and yearned

They would be eating, drinking and resting a while
For when the next journey began it could last many a mile.

In his search for adventure he carried a leather pouch
And when he needed inspiration he would take from it a note

He carried no weapons for he had no need
For his words held wisdom as he had his own creed.

To settle all disputes he would tell a great tale
So nobody got hurt and nobody went to jail

Renowned for his fairness, his courage and his wit
It was clear to see compassion, he had plenty of it

Bringing enemies together by dissolving an old score
Making them good friends fighting no more

At the gates to the castle he often chose to rest
So that all who passed he would gaily address.

An old knight so gallant he never had to fight
His wisdom with words seemed always so right

Adjust Your Thinking Ways

It was a crazy situation
This was no exaggeration
Confusion ruled the day.
It could make your blood boil
To be caught in such turmoil
There must be a better way

Well, if your life is a mess
Then here we must stress
It can all be a delusion.
The way out of this dark cloud
Is to stand up and be proud
Then you start seeing through the illusion

To realize your true worth
Would start to end all the hurt,
Don't think you are stuck in a rut?
To be free of that grey haze
Simply adjust your thinking ways
Then stop acting as if you're a nut

THE IMPOSTERS

This one is about war and how governments persuade young men to go out and kill, destroying innocent nations, all in the name of so-called liberty. They take control of these young men's minds and try to justify all these actions by making the war legal. Perhaps there is a way to cease all wars? Read on ...

The Imposters

The views, opinions and the ideas you stand for
Incite upheaval and are the cause of all war

The sons of darkness, as leaders they masquerade
Enlisting the youth, in false glory they parade

Posing as friendly, dictating falseness and lies
Stealing the spirit of the innocent when they are still boys

Taking the young sons of man, saying it's brave to fight
They prey on their innocence, persuading them that it's right

On TV, they tell us, come join in their game
Contaminating the weak, then spreading the blame

Their actions and deeds cause hell and havoc to others
Why do they not realize, these people are our brothers?

The young and the innocent are collateral damage
In their twisted minds, these people are garbage

☞

Wrecking towns and cities, leaving misery and anguish
When their only crime was they spoke a different language

The children, the innocent, the old and the ill
Why would they think, they have a licence to kill?

Unleashing hell on people who care not for fashion
When their only concern was to find the next ration

With fire in the guts, they attack all around
And nowhere in their hearts is compassion to be found

Those masters of manipulation have taken control of their brain
For now they are robots and close to insane

Masquerading as loyal, the politicians stay at home
You will not find their family in the middle of any war zone

In false glory they return and many made heroes
But in the eyes of the awakened, they are less than zeros

Now it's time for the world to know these imposters
And realize the hell their policies have fostered

Now the moment has come to stop all this madness,
To stop all the killing and stop all the sadness

☞

What would happen today if people start listening
To their spirit inside, as it glows and is glistening?

As the people will grow to acknowledge life
The evils will be found, with no wars to fight

In the eyes of God, there is no place or role
For those that mislead you and steal your soul

As we now approach that special place in time
When God will say, I will take back what is mine

When the evils will be left, all sad and rejected,
Because the spirit of God has been resurrected

As the spirit is discovered and released through the lands,
We can be free and rejoice and bring out the bands

For when we allow this plan to unfold
All war will cease, we'll have broken the mould

Like smoking in public is now out of fashion
The concept of war will have lost all its passion

Now with every dawn, the world will be brighter
And all men will realize it's not right to be a fighter

For at last the world will be a place that is sane
And all who live there now reside in God's name

What Map Are You Reading?

You must have a dream or a wish in your heart
A spark each day that gives you a start

A tiny urge from inside which gives you desire
A picture in your mind telling you to aim higher

Do you ever consider how you got this far?
Can you just realise how lucky you are?

The ideas as a child which you held in your head,
Are you starting to replace with failure instead?

Can you follow that vision which comes from inside?
Can you nurture and grow it and open it wide?

It crosses your mind at least once every day
And with a little effort, you can ask it to stay

Do you have little urges showing you the way?
For if you but listen, maybe start today,

Just follow your impulses and the directions you feel
And you will be given a whole new deal

It's a system for living which comes from within
And the way to know it, well you just begin

Each day as you live, you just let it grow
Then to make right decisions, you will just know

This is the secret which we all need
But what we are taught is more about greed

It's a map or a plan to show us the way
To bring some order to our lives, as we live each day

So if you feel your life is a bit out of tune
You can now restore order and be finished by noon

To live your life with a worthwhile meaning
And to have the life of which you have been dreaming

MONEY

Whatever your status or background, you will appreciate the wisdom in this piece.

Money: the Wise Man's View

Is money just a game? Does it drive people insane?
Do we really understand it at all?
Does it get in the way and lead many people astray?
Can it cause you to take your eye off the ball?

Worthless it really is, yet you need it to do the biz
But do you ever have enough?
Like the donkey chasing the carrot, it can be a bad habit
Turning your life into one big bluff

Don't ever for a second doubt it; you may be better off
    without it
The wise man just sees it as worthless.
For some it's a very big deal as they chase it with much zeal
Often distracting many from their purpose

In dreams of righteousness and wealth, they neglect their
    very own health
For many get in too deep.
But if they only knew what was the perfect thing to do
They could start by stop acting like sheep

The Solution is Obvious

You know when you think and you have got a view
How would you know if it's thought misleading you?

Should your mind be congested with opinions galore?
How would you know the ones you should ignore?

If you are caught in a maze and can't find a way out
Could you ever know if you dropped all doubt?

You may ponder these questions if you must
The solution is obvious, just have more trust

WISE SAYING
If the life you have got is in a bit of a rut
Would you like to turn things around?
To change today to live a new way
Then you start by breaking new ground

Use Your Instruction Manual

Now there is a role or a part for you to play
And your life will be magic, with surprises each day.
So getting yourself in order is what you need to do
And start living your life, the way that is meant for you

Don't let your mind trick you and lead you astray
But 'You can start next week' is what it might say.
For once, just decide and get on the right road
And stop yourself from carrying that heavy load

If you want to be free and have a real life,
A way that is guaranteed to end all the strife,
Seek out your urges and your inclinations too
For they will show you exactly what you are to do

Start to recognize your hunches, make space for them to
   grow
And they will just teach you what you need to know.
And if that old doubt starts to enter your mind
The offers it makes you are far better declined

You will be guided by your feelings all along the way
And once you just listen to them, you can never go astray.
Take control of your destiny and the way you are meant
   to go,
Be guided by what is inside and you will be told what
   you're to know ☞

There is no point in making excuses and leaving things
   pending
Just go with your intuition and find your life will be
   mending.
Don't waste any more time, what are you trying to prove?
Listen more to your heart, then there is only 'the one
   move'

So in future when it comes to making all decisions
You might search your thoughts but go with your
   intuitions
And work with your godly plan, as it pulsates from inside,
Follow your true destiny and always open your heart wide

Where is Norman?

He was the essence of youth as he stood on that green
Today he was made a man, being a soldier was his dream.

His parents so proud, they recalled their only child
The infant they longed for, their affection they had piled

To return their love and make them so proud
He sought out tasks so he'd stand out from the crowd.

To return a hero was the destiny he had sought
And tell tales like his dad of the battles he had fought

Toy guns and cowboy hats were fun and quite thrilling
Nobody considers this could programme him for killing.

Given soldiers as a child, he thought war was just a game
With no thought of the children that he would soon maim

War was fun on his PC, for it sure did amuse
Nobody realised his perception it would confuse

Being told it's for liberty and freedom he would kill
The cost did not matter, there would be no bill

Recruiting young boys, while still in their teens,
Stealing their minds, making them killing machines

Distant lands in the desert, the great battle still raged
Each night in his diary, he'd write and fill each page

In thoughts of his loved ones and those held so dear
Lying awake at night, his tears were all from fear

Telling him it was his job, his mission to complete
And once he remained courageous, he was impossible to defeat

The morning patrol would leave just before dawn
But when they returned some of his colleagues would be gone.

Dispense justice to your enemies, it's for freedom you fight,
Never question your orders, your leaders are always right

Many friends return early, he thinks it's a bit of a drag
But they did not tell him, they went home in a body bag.

Unleashing their missiles, destroying all and sundry
It is legal to kill now, we are not in our country

Infants, young children and grannies are fair game,
Are all branded the enemy so it is they who are to blame.

With just one month more, he's just got to stay alive
Now with two more weeks, he's going to survive

Just one more week, home is his only desire
But the knock on his door told he died by friendly fire.

It was all for a good cause, you should feel so proud
But it did not prevent his mother from crying out loud

While causing such havoc, the leaders stay home,
They will never send their family to any war zone.

Bringing hell to so many, there will be no winner
Staying home where they're safe, toasting war after dinner

What right do they have to decide the fate of so many?
Praying in church on Sunday does seem uncanny.

They justify these wars, telling us it's the solution
Then claiming it's legal, by passing a resolution

Making it now official to cause all this destruction
No thought of compassion, they just followed their instruction.

Wrecking the whole nation, so many cities they spoil
Could it be they just wanted to get their hands on that oil?

What makes these men fight while many are still boys?
Could it all have started when given the wrong toys?

Old soldiers reconsider and many repent,
Regretting with sorrow, to war that they went

Older now, their hearts soften as regret takes its toll
If only they had listened to that voice in their soul.

What's the purpose of living if evil rules your mind?
When you search in your heart, a piece of God you may find

To cherish and grow it, and nurture each day
To guide you to greatness, it will show you the way.

Many poor souls are lost because they were never told
To seek guidance from their heart and stop chasing gold

KNOWLEDGE

The essence of all learning is the level of all knowing and understanding. True knowing results in the expansion of one's faith. To know or to accept one's spirit is, in essence, the ultimate. To accept one's spirit is the key to pure meditation and results in knowledge and learning.

Goodness

If you had goodness in the morning
And goodness late at night,
Would you need any more goodness
Or would everything be just right?

If goodness is just like cream
It always rises to the top.
Could you take a dollop of goodness
If your life was in a flop?

If you needed more goodness
Could you buy it in a store?
But if you made your own goodness
Could you make a little more?

If you had too much goodness
Could you share it with your friends?
Then by giving out this goodness
We could start some whole new trends

Where does goodness come from?
It must be a special gland
Everybody has plenty
But it's in their own unique brand

It's impossible to store it
You must always give it away
And if you're lucky to receive some
It will really make your day

So if you find you have some goodness
Don't keep it for too long
Impart a little everyday
Maybe sing a goodness song

If you have only a little goodness
And you would like a little more
Give away a little goodness
Then you'll find you have goodness galore

What If?

Is there a way to avoid all worry?
Can we live our lives without being in a hurry?
For with all our great effort and all our great plans
Are we part of the problem by sitting on our hands?

We have our beliefs that we think are real
And we even go to war with pride and great zeal.
We take up the mantle for causes so strange
But we have our own destiny that life can arrange

Just see yourself out of that jail,
There are steps you just follow and you cannot fail.
Forget all your plans, your goals and ambitions
And make some space for more premonitions

Your destiny is shaped not by your thoughts
Or the clothes or cars or things you have bought.
Instead it's a wave that comes from within
It's easy to use it; you just have to begin

Take time to care and nurture it slowly
And you will feel free and perhaps even holy.
It will take care of your troubles, and worries just
   leave you
For you will see each day how much they deceive you

☞

Make space in your life for you to enjoy
Those dreams you had when you were a boy.
Gather up all your worries, make a big collection
For now, at last, you're going in the right direction

You're out of the darkness and into the light
For the changes you've made, your future looks bright.
Each day your strength and belief grow stronger
And your cares and troubles are with you no longer

You take up the challenge and follow the cause
And for the sweet things in life, you have time to pause.
You love and appreciate the people around you
For the most perfect life begins to surround you

Your spirit is touched and begins to be freer
For you now begin to be a mystic and seer.
You soon see the world on a different level
Your face looks clear, for you've discarded the devil

Now you begin to live the life of your dreams
For to turn it around was very easy, it seems.
With every day, your new life will unfold
And the secret to freedom you now have been told

Make a Real Change

USUALLY, when people want to make changes in their life rather than make a real change, they just change the scenery. That is, they change their house, their job, their country, their sex, they change everything but themselves. To make a real change in your life, you must delve into the heart of the matter. Be ruthless. Look at your life. See where you are at and see where you want to be. That is, see where in your heart you want to be not where you think you want to be. When you are clear on these two points, where you are and where you want to be, then it is obvious what you have to do to get from point A to point B or so your mind will tell you.

There is another way. Rather than think of where you *should* be, just *be* and have no plans for the future other than doing the 'one move'. The mistake occurs when you think in your mind that it takes thirty years to achieve x, y and z, in which case it does. Real change can be instant when you take the brake off and change the mental filter. Be open to anything. Somebody may walk up to you and give you a million pounds on the spot. Anything can happen when you have an open mind, but many people choose to dwell on their misfortunes and encase themselves in limitations; they simply let their thoughts trick them.

To have real self-expression is to live outside the box, free of mental restrictions. Then anything can happen... even miracles, if the climate allows it.

The Keys to Freedom

What do you think? Does your heart begin to sink
If you listen to the non-believers?
What is their silly game? Are they just lost or insane?
Why do they try to deceive us?

Are they lost in the mist? Have their minds got a twist?
Is it just they have no guidance?
Do they seek self-expression or are they caught in
    depression?
Are they just confused and mindless?

Is it a little odd if you have no desire for God?
What, then, is your purpose for living?
Has your heart turned to stone? Do you constantly
    moan?
And to the world, what are you giving?

And what of your dealings, have you lost all your
    feelings?
Do you have any faith at all?
Can you reach out to a friend? If your mind is rigid, let
    it bend.
What would happen today if you got the call?

Do your thoughts try to trick you, showing you
    pictures that depict you?

Chasing money to solve all your troubles?
So like a fool you respond by chasing rainbows round a pond
Will it take long to burst those bubbles?

So if you want to waste your life going in circles day and night
It's time you had a wakeup call.
Here are the keys to freedom; read aloud so you can hear them,
Soon your problems will be none at all

WISE SAYING
In God people seek but only once a week. What is their intention?
When they leave the chapel they begin to dabble
And of the spirit there is no mention.

Zen Riddle

There was a strange little fellow who would say people are yellow
By refusing to take off their mask,
So he made great plans to stop them sitting on their hands
And he set about his great task

Saying by laws we must abide and there is no need to hide
Your new life it is time to begin
And just for a start seek out what is in your heart
Claiming the secret was always within

He found a little niche on how to make the great switch
He spoke in stories of gold,
In tales of a good life, free of all strife
Saying this new way of living would just unfold

So to improve your lot difficult it is not
Saying whenever you want to begin,
For the people who dare might search everywhere
But the answer is only to be found within

Set Yourself Free

Had we known the truth in our essence of youth
It might have taught us how to live,
For it is never too late to learn to change your state
And teach us how to forgive

To take some advice might add a little spice
And enhance our life each day.
It might change our ways and bring brighter days
And to our path show us the way

Do you have a life full of plenty or is it really half-empty?
Are you just following the mob?
Can you stand out from the crowd and speak aloud?
Or are you just caught in the few bob

It might be a start to look deep into your heart
And explore your very essence
To calm down your mind, for it is only then you may find
You can free your life of nonsense

To uncover your true identity, live your life the way it's
    meant to be,
This is the thrill of living.
To find your right road will lighten that heavy load,
You will realize life is for giving

To find understanding and meaning in a world full of scheming
Is the challenge each day.
As they go about their tasks, the question people should ask
'Am I the cause of my own dismay?'

To find their true role they must listen to their soul,
This is the secret key,
Then they will find they are no longer blind,
It's then they set themselves free

WISE SAYING
Let Wisdom be your system; treasure it in your heart
Use it, never lose it, for it can give you the best head start.

NEWS, NEWS, NEWS
Have you ever noticed that newspapers, news programmes etc. are dominated by bad news? They act as if there is no good news to report. How is this constant bombardment of bad news affecting us? Well, here is one observation.

News, News, News

What if you choose to avoid the news?
Would you miss anything at all?

Because with the news, it brings on the blues
So then you are not on the ball

It is yourself you punish by watching such rubbish
And it's not very good for your state

Drop this desire that takes you into the mire
And start with a clean slate

If you want to improve just make this one move
And see the difference it makes

For we have now said you will have a much clearer head
So stop making the same mistakes

Fickle

The movement of life is strange and fickle
It can present you with situations that just make you tickle

With its ups and downs and highs and lows
So you must be on the ball and sharp on your toes

To be on the right path and fulfill your true role
It is good to have a dream and follow your goal

And if you have days when things seem tough
When you're tired and lost and feel you've had enough

It's just your thoughts that trick you and lead you astray
But stick to your guns then they all fade away

Money

Idiots chase it and many waste it,
Others make it their big goal.
But it's just an illusion, which leads to confusion
So many can end up alone

In strange ways they behave, they can be so naïve,
Some treat as if it were God.
Forsaking their true mission, they can end up just wishing
That their life wasn't so odd

Caught in the illusion and getting full of confusion
When it fails to sweeten their heart,
Having wasted their time living their life out of line,
For peace they must make a new start

What causes them to chase at such a crazy pace?
It often starts with a lack,
So in an effort to be strong, they make decisions that are wrong
They can end up breaking their back

Working day and night in an attempt to express great might,
Trying to show how smart they are.
With such effort all in vain, they end up one big pain
And a life that's just bizarre

Their quest is satisfaction but they have the wrong reaction
And make decisions without wisdom
But with just a little knowledge, they could easily acknowledge
They were using the wrong system

So if you're caught in this net, there is no need to fret
To get your life back in line,
Look into your heart, and then make a new start
And live your life so divine

Keep your head nice and clear so the magic draws near
And seek out your godly tasks.
Go with your intuition and uncover your mission,
For this is what your spirit asks

Then you will find great peace of mind
As your new life begins to unfold
As you make amends, you will appreciate new friends
And the old days will seem so cold

It will seem so odd to have money as a God
And the illusion will soon be dissolved
As you grow in self-worth, you will be free of the hurt
Then your world will have totally revolved

Let the illusion depart, you will find good feelings in your heart
As your destiny is about to begin,
You will grow in great wisdom having discovered the system
Simply by looking within

ARE YOU TRYING TOO HARD TO SUCCEED?

In today's business world, people can be motivated by various ideas. They may put themselves under enormous pressure to succeed. Sadly, in many cases they can be a square peg in a round hole which leads to more pressure and little satisfaction at the end of the day. They can often end up like the donkey chasing the carrot and miss out on life. Read on…

Are You Trying Too Hard to Succeed?

Well, people might say there is only one way
To be a big success
Work hard they encourage, meditation they discourage
Turning their lives into a mess

They delegate, they mediate,
They try to beat the system.
They can't wait, they terminate,
They confiscate all without wisdom

They allocate, they hallucinate
And they even hate the business.
They throw a shape, they indoctrinate
And they have no real interest

They work it up, they stir it up,
They pollute all that is nice.
They eradicate, they're up at eight
And they can't take advice

They procrastinate, they're out the gate,
They are always seen at Mass.
They fluctuate, they hesitate
And it's 'bring on the by-pass'

It's a heart attack, it's a bad back,
It's cholesterol sky high.
They're on the take, it's many a mistake
And then they just die

WISE SAYING
If you live a life and maybe it's not the best
You're tired all day you need lots of rest
You wish and dream for your life to improve
The way out of this maze is to live by the ONE MOVE

The Destiny of Man

Entrenched in one's mind, there is treasure to find
How do you bring it to the surface?

It is the destiny of man to do all he can
For it's his quest to uncover his purpose

Too many will say they will start another day
For it's their thoughts that just trick them

Getting lost in a maze and caught in a craze
Is the only way to depict them

We give you this news so you can now choose
To make a real decision

Don't waste any more time, get your life right in line
Then you can easily proceed with your mission

True Grit (Have you got it?)

Is it wise to disguise
The person who you really are?
In plain old English, can you distinguish?
Or have you gone too far?

Is it mythology or good old geology?
That tells us from whence we came?
Could it be true, that if we only knew
That we are all the same

Do you hold what you have been told?
By the non-believers?
Is it profound, are you sound
Or do they just deceive us?

Can it be said, when you are dead,
There is an eternal part?
For what you have been told and what you have been sold
Or can you feel what is in your heart?

Can you imagine, do you just want to be in fashion
Or do you just think like the mob?
Is it all the same, who is to blame?
Is everybody just chasing the few bob?

Is it just that you are thick, or part of the clique?
Or have you got a soul?
Are you on the case? You don't want egg on your face
Or are you free to stand alone

Why don't you just stop, and don't get into a flop
Or do you just want to hide?
Can you be clear, and stand without fear
And just to listen what is inside?

Have you got grit, or are you just full of it
Are you just holding up walls?
Are you strong and courageous, eager for wages
Have you had too many falls?

Does it sometimes seem, that your dreams
Are moving further away?
Feel them in your heart, which gives them a start
And you will live them one day

If they could stop the clock, would you be in for a shock
Would you like to turn things around?
Have you been hurt, do you seek self- worth?
Do you want to do something profound?

If God were to ask, what of your tasks
What would you like to report?
Could you speak with compassion, and of his love you did ration?
Or would all your good deeds jump forth?

Is your life half empty, and do you seek to have plenty
Of guidance from your spirit?
For were you to know it, you could just grow it
Then a full life you will merit

In your quest for self-expression, it sure is worth a mention
Seek guidance from your soul.
And like a wise chap, it will show you a map
And the destiny that you control

Take your head out of the sand, for once make a stand
To be the person you ought to be.
Where do you think you are going, with the seeds you are sowing?
You will realise it's not 'all about me'

So if you feel a bit strange, is it time to make a change
Maybe you should let God guide you.
If you want to learn what you're missing, you just have to listen
To the spirit that is inside you

The Housewife

The stresses and strains of daily life,
Is there a way free of all this strife?

Just caught in the clutter is so confusing,
My life is a joke but not a bit amusing

Am I going in circles just chasing my tail?
I'm in a poor state, it feels like a jail.

This is not the life I planned so well,
I got what I wanted yet it feels like hell

Each day when I rise I make all my plans,
I've got many duties and too many demands

There are tiny tots and school pickups
And shopping and washing a child with hiccups

A short time ago I was just in my teens
But the life I have now was not part of my dreams.

Now each day rolls by I'm getting more uptight
Something keeps telling me this can not be right

I've got to snap out of it for it feels so wrong
Or I might have a breakdown before too long.

How did I get into such a crazy mess
And why am I under so much stress?

I must find a way out and into a clearing
To live a life that would be so endearing.

I recall as a child I had an inner desire
To follow a path that would take me much higher

But I ran with the mob and followed the trend
Now my world is just pressure, where will it all end?

I am where I am, determined to do the best
And tell the young to follow their quest

So now my children to their hearts I do reach
And tell them their feelings are a form of inner speech,

To search within for their spirit to guide them
And all the wisdom they need is right inside them

Your Wish

If you were given a wish
What would you use it for?
Would you just wish for gold and let your life be sold
For an empty cause

Or could you at last stop being so fast
And use it for another?
Would you let it be or could you see
That's it's yourself you would smother

What would it take to give you a shake,
To jumble up your perception?
Is it always yourself and things like wealth,
Do you never make an exception?

Just how often do you let your heart soften
And feel the life around you?
Just let go of things you know
And let the magic surround you

Who decides the future and the path you should nurture
For your life to have a real purpose?
Do you get an itch to make the switch
And avoid all the torture?

For your life to be blessed, it's best to have addressed
The way you think you should go
And then like magic, when you drop the baggage,
The best direction you will then know

So it's not who you know or the places you go
That will inspire you in your heart.
If you wish to be thrilled and very fulfilled
You just need to make a new start

WISE SAYING
What of the news? It is far better to choose not to watch it
For you have made space but don't put rubbish in its place.
Seek something more cheerful that will not give you an earful,
This will give you a big break, for there are many options to take
and
It is then you are no longer fearful.

IT'S NEVER MY FAULT

This one is for people who find fault with others and are consistently boring people with their problems. They keep ranting off a litany of how other people are the cause of their failures. They speak about people with resentment, jealousy, envy etc. If there is an issue or problem, it's never their fault.

It's Never My Fault

Can you tell if you are caught in a spell
Or are you free to know?
Does it seem you are in a dream
Or stuck in tales of woe?

Are there times when your mind
Is all clouded with opinions?
Are you lost in things like cost
Or is the alarm bell ringing?

Do you know how to go
About putting your life in order?
Is it time to change and maybe rearrange
Before you go much further?

Do you pray and wish each day
For help from above
Or do you make the mistake and just take
From those that you love?

So why can you doubt, with words from your mouth,
The people all around you?
Have you forgot, have you lost the plot
Or is it your thoughts that have bound you?

Are you willing to have your life thrilling?
Then just listen to your soul
For you know, you have only to let go
And this can be your goal

What motivates you in the things you do?
Are they your heart's desire?
Do you have schemes and not your dreams
That you consider higher?

If God were to speak to you for a week
Would you listen to what he might say?
Or would you be a pain and just complain,
Insisting to do it your way?

Are you free so you can just see,
Without any motive or demands?
Or can you accept, with the full depth,
That life has its special plans?

Should intuition, perhaps in a vision,
Help you on your way?
Do you embrace knowledge not taught in a college,
Would it make your day?

Is there a way just to say
How easy it can be?
Should it be your main goal to listen to your soul
And just forget the 'ME'?

Do you hold the view that it is always you
And can it be that you are never wrong?
Must you always be right, are your opinions too tight,
Do you sing the same old song?

Can you just for a while force a little smile
To listen to another person's story?
Forget your pride, open your heart wide
Maybe open a new doorway

So forget who you are and your thoughts so bizarre
And just consider others.
Leave aside your plans and your great demands,
Just accept people as your brothers

Wisdom From Within

If you are troubled with worries which you want no more
Do you seek out a new life that you can adore?

If you think you have troubles and your life is in a mess
Are there some issues that you ought to address?

If you're tired of the cards which you have been dealt
Do you think that life owes you love and great wealth?

Are you really fed up? Do you want to make a change
And all of your life you want to rearrange?

To seek your true destiny and where you ought to be
It's a very big world but it's not all about 'ME'

Hear your spirit inside pulsating each day
Feel what it tells you, for it will show you the way

Your spirit will guide you but you must open your heart
And let it unfold with the whole new chart

So when you get feelings of decisions to make
Look in your heart for which direction to take

And when you are inspired in the form of intuitions
Life maybe just showing you the proper ambitions

It's easy for you to turn your whole life around
For it's the secret to happiness you have just found

Then each time you hear that tiny little voice
Accept its guidance, then you've made the right choice

WISE SAYING
Is there a way to start the day so that everything goes just right?
Yes, there is; for you to whizz, don't eat the previous night.
Stop munching at night and awaken with delight, with energy in the morning
Then you can train without any pain and there will be no need for yawning.

There Are Some

There are some who like to party
Others like rock and roll
There are some who like to work hard
Others just draw the dole

There are some who are into meditation
Others just waste their time
There are some with a burning ambition
Others are all out of line

There are some who will inspire you
Others can be just a pain
There are some who seek out wisdom
Others only want what they can gain

There are some who want to live in harmony
Others try to stir things up
There are some who contribute to life
Others just want to disrupt

There are some who care about the world
Others want to tear things down
There are some who hold it all together
Others just like to act the clown

There are some who can be proud
Others just give up too soon
There are some who are relentless
Others just stay in bed until noon

There are some who stand in the centre
Others just run around in rings
There are some who stay on the bright side
Others just don't realise what life brings

So if you ever feel you have been run over
And you want to get back in the game
You will know not to listen to others
Just listen to yourself because that is the name of the game

The Wisdom in Words

Words that enlighten, words to amaze,
Words that will take you out of the haze

Words that are clever, words which are wise
Words that will help you drop the disguise

Words like wisdom and self-esteem
Now you know what these words mean

Words like spirit, soul and heart
Are very easy for you to impart

Words like courage, strength and wisdom
Are all part of this new system

Words like faith and go with the force
Are an important part of this new course

Words like hunches and intuition
Are very important to a magician

Words like magic and letting go
Are very important for you to know

Words like appreciate and even relish
Are very nice when you want to embellish

Words like stop, maybe and never
Are rarely used by those that are clever

Words like believers, seers and mystics
Can make the writings sound quite artistic

Words like divine, godly and knowledge
Ought to be taught much more in college

Words like smile, words like grin
As we teach you to draw out from within

Words like lessons, words like teach
Words that will help you with your speech

Words that are magic, words that impress
Words that teach you to be at your best

Words like miracles and spiritual healings
Words that help you express your feelings

Words like poems and meditation
Words that give you inspiration

Words like relax and get in line
Can make your life feel so divine

Words like direction and philosophy
Will teach you where you ought to be

Words like visions, which may come in dreams,
Might show you the way or so it seems

Words like secret and unfold
Are used a lot by the wizards of old

Words that encourage and words that entice
Words that can give you good advice

Words like inspire, words that amaze
The magic in words that will teach you new
    ways

Words like worry and even sin
Cease to exist when you search within

All of these words sure do impress
The words of the wizards, which they express,

All of these words help us relate
So that the pupils can grow in belief and faith

Heaven's Game

Up there in heaven they play a game
They try to remember everybody's name

Without any list they begin to recite
And are calling out names till after midnight

So to start this little show
They begin with all the ones they know

Sometimes they have to shout
Taking turns at calling names out

One by one they check them all
Because they are really on the ball

Then as each hour of the day moves along
The list is turned into a song

It's their favourite of all the games
Just being there calling out names

So that when the people finally arrive
They have a place ready since they were alive

Don't ever worry about your spot
Your place is waiting though at times you think it's not

Then as you live your life each day
You may hear the angels as they play

Singing songs and calling out names
Having fun with their favourite games

WISE SAYING

Wisdom is vital information, invaluable to the student who heeds the advice.
Wisdom in the hands of a fool will go nowhere, is valueless; falling on deaf ears, such power is never harnessed. Like the most precious seed in the universe, it never germinates.

The Magic of Ireland

Where wishing wells in abundance are found
To valleys enchanted, with magic all around

Find mysterious rainbows and if you go to the end
There you find more gold than you can ever spend

It has carpets of shamrock carrying a spiritual meaning
Put some in your pocket and of luck you'll be beaming

In their hearts its people, as they bid you good day,
Bless you with magic as you go on your way

It has stories of fairies which cannot be found
But if you walk in the woods, you'll know they're around

You will be touched by its spirit, as you walk by a river
Softening your heart, making you more a giver

Just stand on a hill, and look over the lands
And feel the Spirit flow out through your hands

Let its energy surround you and touch you inside
For if you seek true knowledge, you might want to reside

There is a magical stone for those that seek
To have endless conversations, where once they were meek

☞

Just kiss it once and a wizard you become
But kiss it twice, for it's twice the fun

Enchanted by stories and tales from the past
It has seen many changes, now life seems so fast

The druids and mystics once roamed these lands
And today there is healing by laying of hands

There are tales of a land where you never grow old
Perhaps now is the time for these mysteries to unfold

WISE SAYING
Are there sometimes maybe some people who are indecisive?
Do they have faith? For it is not too late. Why don't they listen to
the wisest?

Get Out Of Your Prison

In chains man exists, trapped in his own mind
So he searches his thoughts, for the key to find

Lost in confusion, he tries in vain
Endlessly searching, causing more pain

Loosing his essence, he is stuck in the illusion
He has lost his talents, by forgetting to use them

Imagine for a moment, if guidance he found
His whole little world, would be turned upside down

For his thoughts misguide him, and lead him astray
But the voice in his heart, will show him the way

Discarding those shackles, which trap his self-worth
Shedding those bonds, ending the hurt

In a tiny voice, that speaks to him daily
A pulsating message, that teaches him gaily

He realises the road, which causes such sorrow
To change direction, would give him freedom tomorrow

Each day of our lives, we do have a choice
To search inside, and find that tiny voice

Ignoring logic, just go with your feeling
Showing you the way, as life gets more appealing

Should you choose logic, to show you the way
It takes you to darkness, and leads you astray

Your thoughts and logic, are one and the same
So if caught in confusion, it's them you should blame

To seek your true destiny, should be your only desire
So follow your impulses, which will take you much higher

Search in your heart, until you get that right feeling
And use this guidance, in all of your dealing

Now you have the secret, to end all the pain
Just ignore logic, it's only for the insane

WISE SAYING
Mostly the hosted are being roasted while being toasted

Hope

Some people seem to get lucky,
Some people follow their dreams,
Some other people have lucky charms,
That is the way that it seems

Some people have magic wishes,
Some people live in hope,
All of this wishing thinking
At times helps some people cope

Some people have marvelous faith,
Some people have strength and courage,
Some people seem to give up too easy,
But this we always discourage

Some people become a bit confused,
Some people they get a little lost,
So to find the way out of this haze
There isn't any cost

So should you have an issue?
Do not churn it over in your mind,
Hold a picture of the final outcome
Then the solution you may find

Who Tells Them They Have Flaws

(For those who want to stop smoking and drinking)

Isn't it funny that something like money
Is what people think they need?
They go out of their way, it can lead them a stray
This is strange indeed

Why do we think so many people drink?
Is it a worthwhile cause?
Are they confused or just being used?
Who tells them they have flaws?

Just to unwind and have a free mind
That is the way out of this confusion.
To be free to see, that it's the powers that be
Who takes advantage and just uses them

It may not be nice to get advice
But if you would like a new start,
Take on a new role and listen to your soul
And feel for what's in your heart

To dissolve the distraction, take some real action,
Some hobbies might bring a change.
You are more fulfilled and you feel quite thrilled
Then your old ways will seem so strange

You don't have to be brave if you want to save
Yourself from the hands you were dealt.
Just like a dream, you are out of that scene
And it sure will improve your health

So take up your book and decide your new look,
The way you want your life to be,
For now it seems stop those silly schemes
Just look in your heart and see

Start to change and begin to arrange,
Then you have a new goal.
It is not a test but do your best
And start to take control

Make this move and your life will improve
And your world gets much lighter.
For you always knew the best way for you,
Your future is now much brighter

So don't delay, just get on your way,
For you have turned your life around.
You can take delight, for it feels so right
And a new freedom you have found

When you are clear, you hold very dear
A desire to help many others,
For you can now show the road they could go
To be free of silly clutters

You will feel so proud as you speak it aloud,
How easy it was to do
To show your new talent, for you are now gallant
You'll feel your life is anew

WISE SAYING
There is a simple mistake, which most people make
They are just reacting to a loss
So they go with the mob and work at the wrong job
Then end up blaming the boss

It's Not All About Me

I tell myself the strangest things,
I yap away pulling all my strings.

I can't do this, I'm bad at that,
I am awake all night, I'm just getting fat

I have so many problems going 'round in my head,
I am tired all day so I just stay in bed.

I tell all my friends my troubles and woes,
I've got to make sure the whole world knows

It seems there's no end to all my cares,
It is advice I seek, but nobody dares

I think it might help so I tell people about them,
It might be very lonely if I were without them

What is the way out of this haze?
I speak to friends but they just gaze.

There must be a way out of this awful hell
Who has the secret for to me they should tell?

How would my world be if I were free of this weight?
It feels kind of good; but hey, just wait,

☞

In those few free moments when I stopped the thinking,
Oh could it be me that makes my life so stinking?

Now as I recall all my troubles
The pain is worse, it may even have doubled.

When I ran for the bus they vanished even more,
 I'm beginning to realise this could be a door

Again at the dentist, they were gone for a while
And in those moments of freedom, I began to smile.

Is it the trick not to dwell on my pain?
Then my freedom again I would regain

To dwell on my troubles is the cause of my anguish,
Like all I had to do was to think in the right language.

I replaced my troubles with dreams from afar
Like winning the lotto and getting a new car

Soon my mind was full of delight
My future looked good, it was getting very bright.

I took a new job, I got off the dole,
Now my life was taking a whole new role

☞

So now, I guide others out of the darkness
And show them the value of themselves to harness.

My life now filled with joy for all to see,
Just remember the secret: it's not always about ME

Never Ever

Do you want to be clever? Then drop the word 'never',
It has too many restrictions.
Don't limit your imagination, use a little exaggeration
Then you can make many more predictions

Discover Your Youth

On the first of January, I said I'd begin
My new resolution and join a gym

Falling into a rut was my greatest fear
So I joined a gym that was big and quite dear

I went most days and trained so well
But my weight and my tummy continued to swell

I thought I'd receive some motivation
But after two months, it was desperation

After each workout, I was tired and confused
And got the impression I was just being used

A big fee I paid for special attention
But the service I got was not worth a mention

Frustrated and annoyed, I packed it all in
For if you join a health club, you just can't win

My weight continued to accelerate each day
I was falling into a rut and losing my way

Then I met a friend who looked ten years younger
Saying that she did it without feeling hunger

She had joined a gym that had a magical touch
Telling me to try it, for she loved it so much

The next day I went to check it all out
I was told I'd succeed, there would be no doubt

Explaining to me, they used special ways
And that I'd have results within 12 days

So I joined for a month, hoping my belt got tighter
But just after four days, I began to get lighter

Ten minutes a day was all it took
Soon I was developing a whole new look

My energy got better, I was feeling so well
So all of my friends I began to tell

The staff knew their business, it was easy to tell
For they changed my body and my mind as well

Then after twelve days, I felt much delight
As I checked the results, I got a fright

Just three hours training spread over 12 days
I looked twelve years younger, I had changed my ways

The freedom I felt after each time I trained
An abundance of energy I had just gained

Everybody remarked that I looked my best
My energy was endless, I was full of zest

To visit this gym I just cannot wait
For the feelings it gives me, they are just great

They explained to me it was the Educo System
And the people who taught it were full of wisdom

WISE SAYING
*Where do ideas come from? Information from meditation
by using intuition
You may see it in a vision in the form of a premonition*

Don't Let Your Thoughts Restrict You

If there were a stone in your shoe and it irritated you
But you didn't bother to take it out,
When you went for a stroll, it might cut a little hole
Then loudly you would shout

Like if you had a sad thought, maybe it's time you
   bought
Into a whole different style.
It's no exaggeration, use your imagination
And have the best dreams you have had in a while

Sometimes when you can't cope and feel a bit of a
   dope,
You might think you're stuck in a rut
But you would change really fast by giving yourself a
   'blast'
And stop acting like a fruit and nut

Fill your head full of your dreams, like you did in your
   teens
Then you are putting the horse before the cart.
The choice is very clear to get your life into gear
And give everything a fresh start

You might think you need a reference to make a big difference
But don't let your mind trick you.
So stop acting the fool and use this one golden rule,
Just don't let your thoughts restrict you

So to be at your best, you only have to rest
Those silly doubts you carry
Live the life of your dreams, avoid all schemes
Then you'll be happier than Larry

WISE SAYING
When you're on a mission, you can be wishing for direction from your soul
So to make a decision, you use your intuition and this is the best way of knowing

The Makings of a Man

Are there some days when we are caught in the haze
And issues pile up around us?
What gives us the feeling? Can our lives have a real meaning
Or do we let our thoughts just bound us?

Is there something in our feelings to guide us in our deal-
    ings
That teaches us to be at our best?
Is there something inside that acts as a guide
That can fill our lives full of zest?

Is there a way of knowing the direction we should be going?
Could we have a built in plan?
Are there secrets to find that we just let unwind,
Could this be the makings of a man?

Is there a part in us that we should just trust?
Can we take direction from the source?
Is there a way to begin to realize what is within?
Can this keep us on the right course?

It is really essential to realise our potential,
It is then all the rules change.
This is the understanding that would cease all demanding
Then our destiny it will arrange

Meditation Speaks On Culture

INTRODUCTION

The concepts of wizards, ancient yoga masters, or perhaps even the whole mystical world of ancient wisdom has been woven through many cultures since ancient times. The following piece is exactly how it came to me word for word. I have no explanation for the piece, other than I sat down to write with a blank page and merely poised the question below. In previous writing sessions, the concept of knights and Jedis came up so I was looking for clarification. Please read on.

Can you explain to us what is a knight or a Jedi when we know them to be one and the same?

OUR UNDERSTANDING is that a knight or Jedi is working from meditation. They have reached a stage of enlightenment where they have connected very strongly to the spirit and they operate in line with that spirit. We use the terms 'knight' or 'Jedi' as symbolic terms. In your world the knight was a hero or a do-gooder, almost like a Robin Hood figure, and the Jedi, as in Yoda, was a wise old wizard who knew how to use 'the force' or magic. These masters operate in both the physical and non-physical dimensions. If you want to view it in terms of religion, the term Archangel might be appropriate. Throughout the ages, they manifested themselves in different forms and have brought many teachings and understandings, which are, today, a distorted part of your culture. Many key discoveries and major culture changes were initially pioneered by these entities.

We are here to teach, guide and take charge of particular events in your world. We sometimes watch in amazement at the folly of your behaviour as you go about your lives, spending your time involved in the farcical nonsense which occupies your lives and your minds. For example, the crazy education system which you put your children through typically lasts fifteen to twenty years and contains a very sorrowful format and content that appears to have been developed by idiots. If you were to choose real education, most teenagers would be wizards and you would have a whole different world within one generation. Your governments are run by clowns. In fact, a clown would do better and the result is that real intelligence is not nurtured, nor is it sought out by the masses.

However, forgive me for rambling on; this is merely to give you an insight, a small insight, into what could really be. That's why we always say, "Follow your destiny, follow your spirit, and let a whole new world unfold." Surely, we don't have to spoon-feed people, as you have learned from the great one. He is constantly saying, "You have part of God inside you now; just, go with your spirit. It will guide you in every aspect of your life." All you have to do is just let it. To do this, to follow the path as laid out by the spirit, is your destiny. In other words, your life will have divine influence. You will make decisions based on intelligence rather than copying anyone. There is no path sweeter than the one that is meant for you; follow it and your life will beam, too. It will help you to avoid all the pitfalls and problems, and you will truly live a life that is blessed. Amen.

MAKE THE CHANGE

Everybody has plans, ambitions and dreams. Everybody desires to change and improve their life. This piece may help you decide to make a permanent change in your life and as a result everything improves.

Make the Change

Have you got style? Do you run a mile?
What are your intentions?

What do you chase? Can you stop the race
And move into new dimensions?

Can you be taught or are you being bought
By illusions that misguide you?

Can you stay cool and learn one rule
And just listen to what's inside you?

Do you spend your day just running away,
Leaving no space for God?

Can you face the truth and begin to uproot
Those feelings which are so odd?

Just drop that frown and begin to calm down,
For you may have a surprise

Get out of that maze and on to better ways,
That will begin to make you wise

If you're unfulfilled and tired of being billed
For a life that you want to change

Find the angel inside, for he is your guide
That will help you to rearrange

Don't make a fuss, get off that bus
If you are heading for the wrong destination

There is only one deed, to change is all you need
And enjoy the new sensation

You can learn to know, it's for the Self to bestow
The direction of your destiny

It may be a surprise, for it comes from the wise
'Just disregard the ME'

Just be clever and don't ever say 'never'
So your life turns to adventure

You've made the right choice, the heavens can rejoice
For then you have a new mentor

There are ways you will find that make it easy to unwind
To live the life of your dreams

You are on the right track, and you will never go back
It's so easy now it seems

You feel much stronger, for then you no longer
Struggle, having stopped all the scheming

As you are uplifted, you feel even gifted
For your life has a new meaning

WISE SAYING
Lonesome is he who has lost his chart,
Foolish is he when he thinks he is smart
Calculating and scheming to outwit his kind
If only he'd learned to use his whole mind

The Cause of Confusion

What starts your day? Is there cause for dismay?
Is it not very exciting?
When it gets going, there is no way of knowing
It could be very enlightened

If you ever felt, that the illusion of wealth
Is the cause of so much confusion?
So why do people chase, almost the entire human race
And get caught in this delusion

There is only one way of knowing, that the direction you are going
Is your perfect path,
To be in line, is really so divine
So you must take direction from your heart

Are you living, but not actually giving
Or contributing to the cause?
If the direction you are going, is not very flowing
Perhaps you should then pause

There is a simple mistake, which most people make,
They are just reacting to a lack
So they go with the mob, and work at the wrong job
A dead end which breaks their back

☞

If they stopped all their scheming and that crazy dreaming,
The haze would begin to clear.
Then the mist would just vanish, all the clutter they could just banish
And then life would be so dear

So if you, too, wanted to start anew
And get your life on the right track,
Start by looking inside, and stop trying to hide,
Then you will not have any lack

Then guidance you can seek, each day of the week,
And you will have made the switch.
No more need to pause, for you will be free of flaws
And a lift to heaven you will have hitched

WISE SAYING
"The cost of honesty does not come cheap," said the thief

IF YOU WERE A CHILD

No matter what society we live in most people will admit that in our modern society there is far too much emphases on money and ownership. This sweet little piece tells us that it is not all about margins or resentments and maybe there should be more attention to attitude and things like compassion and consideration for others. As children we live in a world of innocents and as we grow we pass through the school of hard knocks. So as we mature sadly we become harder and can often end up mistrusting everybody. This piece of writing may cause you to take a fresh look at matters

If You Were A Child

If you were a child, would you go wild
If you could see God
Or would you be told, by people who are old,
To forget that silly thought?

What would you do, if you only knew
There must be another way of living?
For we are never taught that we should have sought
That life is all about giving

Must we always take, be on the make
And be looking out for bargains?
For the deal you have got is worth quite a lot
And it's not all about margins

There is a part in you that is so true
That desires self-expression
But what we were told and what we have been sold,
We were given the wrong impression

So if you have been hurt and you seek self-worth,
There is no need for scheming.
If you want a new start, just look into your heart
And your life will soon be beaming

Stop all the clutter and the resentment you utter
And let your mind begin to clear.
Nurture your affections and thoughts and reflections
And the people you hold so dear

So if your life is in a hurry and you're troubled with worry
And you want to calm things down,
To stop that pace, and get out of that race
And you will never need to frown

It's really up to you what you now do
To change all your future,
Just take your book and begin to take a look
At the things you want to nurture

It will clear your mind and you can unwind
And move into a new understanding,
For at last you can forget the past
Now your true destiny you are commanding

To enrich your life and forget all the strife,
Take guidance from your heart
For you can enjoy, you feel on a high
Once you have made a new start

SEEK FULFILMENT

Have you ever felt empty or unfulfilled? Have you ever felt like a square peg in a round hole? It has often been said that everybody has a true role or destiny which they are meant to follow and should we choose otherwise we can end up lost, feeling empty or unfulfilled. However should we choose to move more in the right direction, everything improves. So how do we know what is the right direction? That's exactly what this piece is about....

Seek Fulfilment

There is a way and a reason to live,
For life to teach you how to just give
Then there is a meaning to all your deeds.
Can you feel for others and their needs?

Old men might say, in time they do mellow
And if you listen to your heart, you're a very wise fellow.
What purpose do you serve if you don't serve God
Or do you choose to live a life so odd?

Is it now time to stop all the racing?
Maybe it's your duties you should be chasing?
Then your life has fulfilled a worthwhile meaning
So there is no need to be caught up in scheming

Take a look inside for the wizard within
Then a whole new world you will begin.
Seek out wisdom and act on your premonitions
Then you are directed to more godly missions

Hold your head high and walk so proud,
Go speak of your role and do it aloud.
Take stock of your life and keep out of the haze
Then your world is filled with magical days

For your life to improve without costing a penny,
Don't search for other ways, there just aren't any.
Seek out the direction that's buried deep within
Then your whole new life is about to begin

WISE SAYING
What is it so close that helps us the most,
What gives us a burning desire?
What helps us along when things go wrong,
What gives us the life we admire?

Where Is the Real You?

What do you do
When you don't know what to do?
Because if you only knew
The things you were to do
For it's yourself you would renew

If you want to be anew
The changes are very few,
Then you do what you are to do
Because then you are being true
To what you are meant to do

So if you are feeling blue
And you know it's not you,
Maybe it's something you have to go through?
Then you realise
That life works for you too.

So when you just do
What you are really meant to do,
It brings out the real you.
For only then you are really true
To the spirit inside you

Billy

It was a remarkable day as the band started to play,
This was to be a great day for Billy.
Standing there he began to tremble, for him it did resemble
An event that was meaningless and silly

It was totally without compassion to be honored in such
    fashion
As his whole heart filled with regret,
Feeling it was not very thrilling to be involved in such killing
As he stood there he began to sweat

He felt it very odd as the crowd did loudly applaud,
To him it was not very brave.
No medal he desired for those shots that he had fired
Sending a young boy to an early grave

He was still in much shock shooting a child that threw a rock,
Being told he must follow orders.
Thinking that poor little soul, he never asked for that wicked
    role
All in the name of disputed borders

He found it all very odd, both sides believing in God,
Yet they were hell bent on destroying each other.
When he pictured that little lad he felt sick and really bad
Wondering what it was like for the child's mother

Who could really gain from a war that's just insane?
All this in the name of a piece of land.
Then everybody will deny why so many had to die
In his ear he could hear the marching band

As his turn was drawing near he began to shed a little tear
Sadness and regret filled his mind.
What child would not pick up a stone when they destroyed his family home?
Why are the leaders so blind?

As he walked out on that stage being honored for killing at such a young age,
He was not going to join their phony parade.
For he too had a young son which reminded him of what he had done,
It was now time to end the masquerade

Taking the mic in his hand he felt for once he should make a stand,
What he was about to do would take real courage.
The war that they had planned, celebrated by the marching band,
All other young men he was going to discourage

There would be no celebration in handing him his decoration,
Shooting children was not part of his dream,
The leaders who endorse such acts remain safe in their packs
Drumming up their next evil scheme

Saying he was not one bit proud as he began addressing the crowd,
Explaining war does not make a man brave
And he was no longer willing to hold up arms to civilians
Think of the many they would save

Asking were they all so dense, it was now time to make some sense
And live their lives so clean and pure.
The leaders are so insane, wasting precious life down the drain
And acting like their head was in a sewer

The politicians stay at home safe from any war zone,
Ordering their soldiers to create hell,
Wrecking city and town bringing every home down
Are their minds caught in an evil spell?

To the sound of the marching band, he took the medal in his hand
And fired it high up into the air.
By following their instruction it caused too much destruction
For their stupidity he did not care

It just was not right to be involved in such a fight,
In war nobody can win.
There was too much sadness to be involved in such madness
It was all too much of a sin

Telling those folks to pray, Billy was led away,
His outburst would send him to jail.
Then something very odd as the crowd began to applaud
And Billy knew he did not fail

Then there was a report when later he appeared in court,
His protest had outraged those in power.
Many people gathered outside for they too refused to hide,
For the leaders it was all turning sour

The crowd began to swell and it was plain to tell
That they wanted Billy set free.
Those in power had no choice, for the crowd had one big
     voice
And that was exactly the way it was to be

Determined to do his best, it became his great quest
To tell the world to cease this madness.
Nobody had the right to send those young men to fight
It was all just too much badness

If you want to be brave just think of all the children you
     would save,
Isn't it about time you stood out from the crowd?
When you do what is right you sleep much better at night
And you are free to stand up and be truly proud

Make the Right Connection

Now imagine if you can the pure essence within man
And how his spirit guides him,
For to listen to his soul should be his big goal
And take guidance from what's inside him

It would open his heart and make him very smart
And change his whole understanding.
It would give him a view to make him anew
And live a life that was just outstanding

Then realizing his unique role would give him a real goal
So he no longer searches in the dark.
Giving his life a real purpose, never again to feel worthless
All it takes is one tiny spark

It is then he is gallant, knowing he has got a real talent,
That he is living with a whole new direction.
His vision is much clearer as his destiny draws nearer
Just by making the right connection

The Rat Race

What is this rat race to accumulate money?
For to only consider it, it might seem very funny

Going around in circles making lots of noise
Just to appear sharp and to be one of the boys

We can even get ruthless when doing our job
Is this all because just to make a few bob

It can seem so tragic to be caught in this net
It can send us into a panic and cause us to fret

So if you are so wise yet you are stuck on this treadmill
You say you must do it just to pay the bread bill

If you have these delusions let us be honest for once
To persist on chasing rainbows you might end up a dunce

So if it is your intention to stash all you can
Maybe it is time you woke up and became a real man?

Is your world too confused, is your mind running crazies?
Is it better to realize now and not when you are pushing
   up daisies?

What pictures do hold, do you have the right vision?
Could it be the case that you have a very different
   mission?

Do you think you were put on this earth to accumulate
   gold?
Your destiny is quite different, are you now ready to let
   it unfold?

WISE SAYING
If you're in a haze or a bit of a daze,
In a place you do not belong
Without any doubt, there is a way out,
But you must learn where you went wrong

There Is

There is good, there is bad, there is happy, there is sad
There is love, there is hate, there is doubt, there is faith

There is swear, there is prayer, there is need and there is care
There is lost, there is found, there is silence, there is sound

There is fear, there is joy, there is low, then there is high
There is sickness, there is health, there is poor, there is wealth

There is young, there is old, there is good, there is bold
There is many, there are few, there is a spirit within you

WISE SAYING
Rich is the man who has godly desires
Proud is the man whose word inspires

The Wizard

If man could only see what he was really meant to be
And realised his true potential.
To know his true worth would free him of all the hurt
But to clear his mind it would be essential

To know of reality would fill him with vitality
And to understand his connection with God,
Then it's a whole new scene as he becomes a real being
And ceases living a life so odd

So instead of just wishing, he will understand his mission
And lives the life he was destined to live.
This is not very strange as his spirit brings great change
Then his one desire is just to give

Free of all distraction, his world is not based on reaction
And he never delves into bad news.
His passion is then strong to help those who are living wrong,
It is always the right road does choose

Like the wise men of old he has broken the mould,
He has rid his mind of all kinds of doubt,
Showing others the way to free them from their dismay
It is always the right road he will choose

Bad thoughts don't affect him for he will not reflect them
He refuses to pollute the minds of others
Not conned by delusions he sees through the illusions
He seeks to unite all his brothers

As he treads his golden road, those who meet him are bestowed
With the knowledge to give them a free mind.
As the wise man would say he would surely make your day
And increase your faith in all of mankind

So the secret to true awareness is your own spirit you harness
Then a new way of living you begin.
Then the choice is very clear as your destiny draws near
By taking guidance and direction from within

WISE SAYING
Blessed is he who seeks a life so divine
Holy is he if his spirit he does mine

Words to Enlighten

Words to impart, words to touch your heart,
Words to guide the way,
Words to choose, words that bring good news,
Words to make your day

Words to enlighten, words to take delight in,
Words to tell you the truth,
Words to stir up, words that shake up,
Words to bad habits uproot

Words to let you know, words to let you grow,
Words to cause a resurrection,
Words to suggest, words to fill you with zest,
Words to grow into a collection

Words to renew, words just meant for you,
Words to give you a smile,
Words to grow your feelings, words to give meanings,
Words to give you style

Words to teach, words that will reach,
Words to bless all who see them,
Words to set us free, words that make us see,
Words to heal all who read them

DEFINITIONS OF WORDS USED IN THIS BOOK

Here is a brief explanation of some of the terms featured in the writings:

God: He is often referred to as Life or Self.

The 'Me' or the 'I': This is the personality or ego. Most people confuse the personality with the true essence of the person. The personality is like an overcoat we wear, very often shrouding our true self. One of the purposes of meditation is to nurture the self and allow it to express itself unto the world.

Soul or spirit: This is often referred to as the part of God that is inside you.

Energy: People who attend healing or prayer meetings will often speak of feeling Energy. It may flow from the healer or the individual attending the healing session. It is said that this energy is what brings about great cures and will often cause the individual to seek a real meaning to their life.

A Blast: In short, this is when a healer allows the energy to flow out from his/her hands; the patient can feel it in the form of a Blast (or a surge of Energy).

Yoda, Jedi: In the Star Wars movies, there is a character who was in essence a wizard or wise one. He is very psychic and he understands the Force. He is a lovable puppet character called Yoda. One of his jobs is to teach particular individuals how to use the Force/Magic to the level of a Jedi master.

The One Move:	Means to focus all your attention on what is happening right now, to centre your awareness in the present moment. The purpose of the one move is to stop the 'normal' hyperactivity of the mind, by using all the senses to focus in the present e.g. what am I seeing, hearing, and feeling right now? Much of yoga training is devoted to helping the student to develop the capacity to be 'one-pointed' by paying attention to the breath or the movement of the body. Similarily, in the Zen monasteries, the monks trained to focus on the present task e.g. sweeping the floor, and not on the end result, the clean floor, or on what to do after the floor is cleaned. Modern psychology often refers to this state of being fully engaged in what you are doing now as being in the *flow*. Champions in any field, whether it be sport or music, often refer to a peak state they call being in the *zone* where they are not aware of anything other than the music or whatever activity they are involved in. It is often at such times that they give their best performance.
Mankind:	Frequently where the word 'man' or 'mankind' is used in these writings it refers to all of human kind, that is both men and women.

Notes

Notes

Notes

Notes

Notes

Notes

Notes

Notes

CPSIA information can be obtained
at www.ICGtesting.com
Printed in the USA
BVHW011530080121
597358BV00006B/277